How to Be the Best Intern in the World

Brandon K. Hoffmann

Copyright © 2020 by Brandon Hoffmann

Cover Art designed by Les (GermanCreative)

Published in the United States by KDP by Amazon.

ISBN 978-0-578-64565-0

Library of Congress Cataloging-in-Publication Data has been applied for.

FIRST EDITION

To all the current and future interns around the world.

Employers, please treat them right.

Contents

Foreword

By
Devin Graham
CEO of Devin Super Tramp, LLC

Experience is essential to the workplace. Our success as a company is due to hiring experienced, passionate, hard-working people. The best way to learn any job is simply doing it. Sometimes it means you'll have to start at the bottom; most people don't start out as CEO on day one. Rather, the people who receive serious opportunities are those who prove themselves through hard work. When I applied to my university's film program, I was rejected the first time.

From that moment on I was determined to prove myself. I volunteered on every project, no matter how big or small. Often, I would find myself in charge of cooking food for all the other film-set employees, just so I could have a place on set. By putting in my time, proving to people I would do whatever it takes, and committing those 1000 hours of doing intern work, it created so many incredible opportunities for me.

When I set out to become a filmmaker, the first step I took was to research the most well-known filmmaker in the area. After receiving his email from a college professor, I wrote to him explaining I wanted to work for free. He responded and told me to show up on set the following day with a Snickers candy bar for him ready to work. I showed up with a King-Size Snickers.

From that moment on, I made sure to work harder than anyone else on set. I would be the first to arrive and the last to leave. I would clean up the messes no one else would. I became invaluable. Soon enough, I was asked to help on every set. From there, I started to get paid offers from the same people who originally had me work for free. Starting off this way in my line of work was the only way I could have found the success I now have.

My success was founded on hard work, and I have lived the full experience. I wish someone could have put it this simply when I was beginning my professional career. I embraced the six principles mentioned in this book to improve and I am confident that anyone who takes these steps seriously will stand out from every other intern in the company. Doors will open and future possibilities will present themselves, creating endless opportunities. I am living proof it works.

-Devin Graham

Notes/Doodle Page

PREFACE

It was December 2019 and I was strolling back into the wondrous office I called home after a nice holiday break. With only two days to spare between the holiday season and the New Year's break, I questioned the priority of the tasks I should undertake. I took my time wandering through the (once-thought numerous but now-known) few emails waiting in my inbox, placing them in the neat digital folders I created in my attempt to stay organized.

When I started my new job only 45 days earlier, I was introduced to a large supply room filled with every kind of office supply one could imagine, from organization tools to crisp clean paper boxes; it was a childhood dream come true. I was entranced, but there was one small thing that bothered me: the windowless room was in a bit of a flurry. Everything had a place, but nothing was quite as "neat" as it could be. My immediate thought was to clean it, but not knowing the full responsibilities of the position, I tucked the idea away to the place where memories are stored for the future, writing on my pink sticky note "Copy Room" to remind me of the future task.

The time came 45 days later, when I found some "in-between the holidays" time to finally brush up the copy-supply room. I opened the door to the room, placed the recycle bin as a doorstop, and began the pink sticky-note-reminded cleaning of the "Copy Room." As silly as this sounds, it was a day I anticipated on each of the many days I walked in and out of the room. Though I assumed the feeling of excitement and thrill would allow me to work hard and quickly accomplish the awaited task, I began to fume with anger. Frustration filled my thoughts as I went through boxes of random papers and folder organizers. From my frustration, the idea of this quick read began to fill my mind (with the title included) front and center on my noggin. The imagined book read (in big bold letters, mind you): "How To Be the Best Intern in the World." It was a short book, and I imagined it as one of those stocking stuffers for those around my age, specifically the newly graduated who were using internships to launch their careers.

Interning was the name of the game when I first got on to the career path I always thought was my dream job. It really was the best way to navigate the creative world of commercial video advertising. I had many discussions with those in this world who told me experience was key, so I took that key and found my lock. The love of learning from those I would consider experts in their craft enthralled me. I wanted to know all they had gained from a life focused in making creative products and interning was the perfect way to do it.

Although it seems an unexpected connection, finding myself later as an executive assistant in the delightful organization I now work for, I drew from my experience as an intern working on commercial video sets and found that it prepared me to work for my current employer in Washington, D.C. where my passion currently lies.

No, this is not a business professional book. I'm just one guy pulling from my experience in the angered fashion of cleaning a supply room who decided to share my thoughts with you on how you can be the best intern a company could ask for. Take it or leave it, neither of us has anything to lose, right?

Anyway, let's amuse one another and continue this journey together. I'll share what I've learned and then you can write some notes in the margin on what

you learn. Maybe one day we'll combine our thoughts
and create the:

"Ultimate Guide to Interning Anywhere."

Now, I'm going to assume you're at a crossroads
in your life: either you have an internship, are looking
to find one, or your parents gave you this book
hoping you'll be able to do something with your life
and maybe they think an internship is a good place to
start. You are about to embark on a journey where
life is going to continue to give you crossroads like
the one before you now. Truly, it takes a lot of
courage. The benefit of any internship is not only the
experience and resume-building; it's also about
refining the idea of what you want to find in the place
the world often refers to as a "job." I thought for the

longest time I wanted to be a "filmmaker" (very broad right?), so I interned in the world of creating videos and eventually was hired into a position some would call a "filmmaker" (technically, my W2 stated I was an editor, but as the company expanded I took on more roles). Taking the wisdom I learned as an intern, I became an ever-improving editor. With this new ability, I was assigned to create social media content and with those skills I found success as a social media content creator. I had envisioned a career as a filmmaker but refined my desire within a more specific capacity. When I began to specialize and hone my skillset I found a passion for a career I hadn't quite imagined in the fast-paced world of social media content. As I saw the decline in the video analytics and social-reach numbers of what I considered to be "successful," I formed a new desire to take on a producer role where I could focus on the logistics of preparing a film shoot and planning for the director's vision. This led me to gain expertise on the logistics and planning side of production, paving a pathway into my move to Washington, D.C. to become an executive assistant, where a lot of my day includes logistics and planning for the schedules of executives.

Strangely enough, the skills gained from intern to current career have redefined my "dream job" and I accept the possibility I will forever be chasing the "perfect" fit. Luckily, I feel pretty good chasing this dream. All I'm trying to say about my own life is these internships help direct you to seeking a rewarding and fulfilling career path, traditional or non-traditional. It will take a lot of patience to truly find the ideal position so allow your thoughts to evolve as you develop your idea of a "dream job".

Now back to the business: if you've chosen to make an internship part of your life journey, what can I tell you about how to succeed? From my utterly short time on earth, with freshly created memories, here are my top 6 steps to be the best intern in the world. (Quick note if you haven't noticed: I like extremes, so I will be referring to the title of this book with all of the exaggerated glory it deserves.)

1. Clean and Organize Your New Office Space – From Desk to Storage Room

2. Volunteer for Everything

3. Get to Know Every Individual (Not Just Their Latte Order)

4. Do the Dirty Work

5. Find your Niche

6. Become an Asset

I'm no business man (that's why I asked one to write the foreword), so let's have a candid conversation and I'll let your biology professor survive in your psyche as the lecturer.

Chapter 1:

Clean and Organize Your New Office Space - From Desk to Storage Room

Ask yourself: Are you surprised why this random idea resides at the beginning of our discussion, first and foremost? Let me explain myself and help you understand why this small and simple feat can make a great impression on your new colleagues.

Whenever I begin a new position, I often wonder where to find everything. Where can I get paper, pens, notebooks, computer charging cords, copy and printer supplies, and all the other essential and unexpected items I may need to be successful? Where are my tools for success? Companies often have procedures and an organizational structure to accomplish their work. Why not combine an understanding of this with locating the tools needed by cleaning and organizing the office? Think about this: If you don't know where anything is, wouldn't it be easier to find out early in your internship rather than trying to search through everything to find it only when you actually need it? I've found in the fast-paced world of many internships that trying to find essential items can be frustrating and needlessly time-consuming. I'm not saying this is a must-do item from day one, but it is a great way to show your work ethic.

When I started my current position as an executive assistant, I was given a tour of the building and the office; it was a quick run through and I retained very little information. The only thing that really stuck out was how much opportunity there was to clean and organize.

The individuals you'll be working with will have an established routine. They will be set in their own ways of doing things. Therefore, as you're looking for an opportunity to get organized, take this step cautiously and ask before starting anything. When you receive the green light, I'd encourage you not to take up precious work hours to clean and organize but rather stay late or come in on a weekend to work on an area or a room. Label everything precisely, make a physical inventory, and keep things in the same general area as before, so as not to confuse your tenured colleagues. When you clean and organize, you'll begin to find out what products the company has, you'll know where things go, and you'll make a quality impression on the whole office.

One of the positive side effects found while opening my internship with this step was having employees and executives alike come to me asking if I had seen a certain item they needed. Because I had a mental and physical inventory, I had key information many of the other staff did not have. This gave me more opportunities for face time with executives and colleagues who I could one day be asking for a permanent position. When they see the initiative and work ethic portrayed in your actions, it

often leads to more opportunities and faster growth.

Those who are the decision-makers see your

potential and it increases your capability to become a

vital asset to the organization and the people who run

it. When you're done with the supply room, ask to

move on to the next area of the office. It's a simple,

yet highly effective feat, so why not try it out?

Chapter 2:

Volunteer for Everything (Professionally)

While you're out and about cleaning the different

office spaces, why not get involved? During most of

your internship you will be volun-told to do all sorts of

tasks. For some it's latte orders, for others it's making

lunch reservations, and for still others it's writing and

writing endlessly. There will be tasks you like and

other you don't; nearly all things come with positives

and negatives. Keep in mind, as an intern, this time is

all about refining and redefining your job or career criteria. Volunteering for everything will give you a unique perspective into other unsuspecting parts of the job. Who knows, you may find something you never imagined to be enjoyable. If there's an event, volunteer to help. If there's a luncheon, volunteer to order the catering. Get involved and be involved.

I remember a time when I was interning on a film shoot and the brand new 360-degree videos were being tested. When the shoot ended, I immediately volunteered to help on any further projects. A few weeks later, the owner of the company asked if I wanted to take on the 360 project and learn the software for him. I was so delighted I went right to work. I learned the new software, stitched 6 camera images together, and put all my free time into creating the visual piece. Although I wouldn't necessarily recommend this, I hired a guy to come and help me color the footage; I was trying to take my volunteering to the next level. When the director returned two weeks later, I gave him the finished footage that he was then able to send to the musician to score. It was during this time I gained an unimaginable opportunity that propelled my knowledge and helped me develop an unexpected skillset. As I thought about this, I realized it wasn't just about volunteering, it was about an experience that provided me with new skills I would not have obtained otherwise.

Often, even as a regular employee, I'll volunteer for after-hours events when I'm available. This is beneficial as I get to know other colleagues better, meet new people I would have otherwise never met, and experience food, places, and cultures I might have never known about. My encouragement even goes as far to say: volunteer for the boring meetings no one else wants to attend. You never know, there might be free food!

Hard work usually pays off, and even when it doesn't, you learn something. Be eager to engage and eager to try. Volunteer to assist at a sporting event. Volunteer to clean out the office of a departing employee, volunteer to hold the doors at a reception, even volunteer to read or rewrite the policy manual.

Just volunteer to help the company improve – this in and of itself is a valuable asset. Think about how much more knowledge you can acquire when you offer to help. Set yourself up for success by volunteering for everything.

Chapter 3:
Get to Know Every Individual
(Not just their Latte Order)

This chapter is pretty self-explanatory and to the point. I hope you were raised believing everyone deserves to be treated with dignity and respect. If this is the case, let me assure you we are on the same page and maybe add a few new ideas to your pot. Remember, you are going to have time to get to know those who are relevant to your job, but what about the others? What about the custodial staff; what about every other person you pass in the hallways, on the elevators, and at events? Are you treating everyone with respect and dignity? This is the time to start or continue whatever life-kindness habit you've acquired. (If you forget, just remember the golden rule.)

You are going to be dealing with a lot of different personalities, so be ready. Some will give you one-word answers and some will explain the finest details. Some are courteous enough to smile and some may not even acknowledge you. Each individual will appreciate something different so always be looking for ways to adapt and change your approach. We all have a unique way we'd like to be acknowledged and it can vary by culture, personality, and style. Get to know birthdays, likes and dislikes, even hopes and dreams. Evaluate the differences between each individual and note that personalities vary wide and far. Most importantly, always be kind. And, even if you're having trouble putting on a smile, you can always be polite.

When I was in my teenage years, I worked as a "custodian" (they called us "facilities managers") at a local theater. At only 15-years old, it was an amazing opportunity to get my first direct-deposit paychecks; I was ecstatic. The only two things I did each day to prepare for the 4:00 pm shift were changing into my colorful company-logoed T-shirt and placing my building keys in my pocket (the best part about facilities management is you can access almost every room in the building). It was a bigger change than I could have imagined. For most of the day I was a friendly high school student and cross-country runner, but when 4:00 pm rolled around, it felt like people changed their view of me. It was an interesting shift in public perception and all I did was change my shirt. Luckily, my co-workers and colleagues treated me in a similar fashion to everyone else. It was often with the public that it was more noticeable. Now, keep in mind, I was that one guy who always said hello to everyone, customers and employees alike.

When I walked out of the custodial closet with my trash can drum and cleaning supplies, I received a lot fewer "hellos" and "how are you's" than when I would walk in. Instead, many just turned their eyes away. I became very curious about this, so I decided to test out a few things to see if I could get a different reaction. I walked around in my normal clothes saying hello to everyone and, in response, hellos were returned. A few hours later, I would walk around with my cleaning supplies and, even after I said the same hellos, I found that they were rarely returned. Truthfully, from my experience, the eye turning became a lot more common. Either way I was still me, but I can honestly say I did not feel treated the same way. If you've ever watched the show "Undercover Boss," you'll know what I mean. Reserve some thought for reflection on my experience next time you're in the office and you pass different employees in the hallway. Do you reach out with the same courtesy to the custodial staff as you do to your office manager?

The main message I want to impart is this –
whether at work or home, park or college, be kind.
From executive to educator to electrician, treat
everyone with respect and dignity. Whether you love
or hate being "that guy," from the concierge to the
custodian, get to know them all. I encourage you to
smile and give a hello for everyone you meet. Who
knows, you may find a new best friend or another
fortuity?

Chapter 4:
Do the Dirty Work

Let's be honest with ourselves, you've been doing the dirty work for a long time. Papers, readings, study, you name it, you've done it. Now is the time to take the dirty work of academia and show the world you can apply it in the workplace. Cleaning and filing paperwork is no longer a waste of time. You are a gatekeeper of the organization, creating the ease of finding documents and materials for your colleague and client needs. Every moment you spend in the office increasing profit margins is no longer costing you money; rather, it's bringing your financial pocketbook into the green (creating an income and positive cash flow). Mentally, it's comforting to know that money is no longer walking out of your pocket. Now is the time to step up, stop playing games, and get to work. "Winging it" is no longer an option. You now have the company's interests on your shoulders and there's no time to slack off or procrastinate. It's time to jump in and become a sponge of information and a facilitator of functioning.

So far, we've discussed the essence of organization, volunteering, and getting to know other individuals. It's time to put it all together and test it out. When you volunteer for that event, you show up (early), help out, and clean up. Nothing, and I mean nothing, is beneath you. If you grew up with a maid, you are now that maid. Every task assigned to you, do it with an educational mindset. Ask yourself: "What can I learn from writing this paper, briefing report or memo on [insert subject here]?" "How can I show my colleagues my best work?" "Who can I assist today to help my company be better than it was last week?" Everything is on the table here. A friend once told me to think proactively and take initiative so when there are moments of free time you can request additional "dirty work," contributing your help. I think this sums up a good chunk of being the "intern." Think ahead, anticipate change, be on your toes, and never stop looking for education. If you put in the best work, which comes with optimal effort, you will get the best results.

As much as I wish I didn't drain my mental capacity thinking about the "pecking order" mindset of workplaces, I have often felt that in some companies it can't be avoided because the vertical workplace is largely a myth. Therefore, since you have little control over where you are in the pecking order, you have to find a way to control your destiny. This is where doing the little things, such as the dirty work, come into play. The more willing you are to do the little things that contribute to your organization's success, the more respect and trust you receive (unless it's broken by another circumstance). And don't forget that this takes time – growth and respect increase over time.

As you do the dirty work, you must be patient and understanding. Standing out as an effective and efficient worker is key in this stage. You can "teacher's pet" a senior at your company all you want, but until you produce some proven results, you won't get very far.

We all start one way or another. When you get your feet wet, it shows. Some people think "oh I'll do the dirty work now and it will lead me to doing the easy work later." But here's the thing: the dirty work gets easier as you become better at it. Maybe you never stop doing the dirty work, maybe it will feel less dirty as you gain experience? Think about the boss of the company. There's a good chance she or he started where you are, but because they became so good at the dirty work, it was no longer "dirty." Experience made it easier. Suddenly, the work was no longer as hard and laborious. They became a professional at their job, finding ways to use their time more efficiently.

If you can't tell from the beginning, I enjoy cleaning. The first time I clean a room, or especially an entire house, it's mentally brutal because it's all so unknown. As I become more familiar with the layout, I start to know where everything goes and determine the process I'm going to pursue to accomplish my desired outcome (i.e. clean and organized home). I start to see how things are placed, guiding me to form a dynamic and systematic process. Did anything change? Not really, but I'm now more experienced and I know how to do the job better. Part of shifting out of the dirty work mindset is ending the self-created definition of the term "dirty work." And I guarantee that as you take this approach, you will start to see every task as a disciplined study.

Think about the satisfaction of learning something new every single day! Change your mindset on the thought of "dirty work" and be able to see with increased clarity the important effort moving the company forward. See a purpose in all the work you do, big or small, for the change or improvement of the organization. This will aid in finding your place within. When you think you've found your "niche," become the expert in it. Allow your mind to be consumed with your niche, permitting your understanding and talents to flourish.

Do the dirty work, find what you enjoy, and discover how to become a contributor to your team. This will enhance the pursuit to your eventual goal of becoming the kind of person colleagues crave to hire full-time.

Chapter 5:
Find Your Niche

Finding your place in the company is a journey that requires a lot of patience. With a degree or certification, you may already know what department you will intern with. Over time, however, as employers see your style of work, personality, and interests, you may end up in an unforeseen role. As you move forward with your internship thoughtfully discuss your interests and desires with your potential employer. Communicate openly the path you see your future taking, allowing both parties to envision a good fit in the organization.

This chapter is all about finding an area to shine. You may hate cleaning and love writing (opposite of me), but let's say your job as an "intern" involves both. There is no reason you must learn to like both. As you blossom in your new role, the potential employer will see what fits, developing a sense of your niche or where you could potentially bring the most value to the company. Importantly, build yourself into the groundwork of the company and make what you know valuable. In chapter one, I mentioned a quick and easy way I found to become valuable: knowing where stuff is. To this day, I still get calls from my previous employer asking where a distinct item may be. It's great to feel needed.

Finding your passion may take months or even years, but don't rush it. Try everything, be the first to volunteer. You may have despised writing papers in college, but if the subject matter is law and social services, you may find joy writing on the clear-cut subject. Don't discount any experience, as each will help you find your niche. You may not fit the mold of one company but remember there are thousands to choose from. Understand that showing true professionalism in the workplace will bring more respect from your colleagues and proof you can work with them. As I'm writing this, I'm discovering more of what I like and don't like about each job or task, and it's honestly all right if the cycle never ends. Use this opportunity as an intern to mold your niche. Find a job in the company that generally fits you, instead of trying to fit their mold (but still be willing to be "moldable"). I can promise more happiness when your career is something you find a sense of joy in.

Chapter 6:
Become an Asset

Why are you even needed? Many people misconstrue that interns are hired to do the work no one else wants to do. Sometimes they are, but are you? If you want to feel or actually be needed at this company, simply become an asset. Become irreplaceable.

Frankly, everyone is replaceable. If this is true, then ask yourself, what are companies paying you for? Think about how much money it would cost an employer to hire a different person all the time for the same job. You're a professional because you're willing to become an expert in a job the company needs to fill in order to accomplish its mission.

Starting from the intern role, you're going to learn the most basic skills the company needs – the most easily replaceable skills. As you grow each day, you're gaining new-found knowledge that will one day put you ahead of every other person they "could" hire. Think about where you want to end up, whether in this company or another. Do you want to be at the top? Executives get paid the big bucks because the pressure and risks are on them. Wouldn't it be interesting to be an expert in something other than attempting to rise to the top? Too many people are chasing that dream anyway! Do the hard work it takes to become an expert in a unique field. Rather than chase the rise, chase the hard work.

No matter what you do, become the expert. Let's say you clean toilets; become the expert. Here's an idea: know all of the cleaning solutions, the best and the worst and why; know the ingredients; and know how to save someone from inhaling those ingredients.

By continuing to learn and improve, you propel yourself ahead of other talent. When you started this journey, you had the same knowledge as each classmate (okay, maybe not exactly but let's say you took all the same classes so generally speaking). With each passing day you work on something new (a brand-new problem). With each new experience comes a unique route to solving the "problem," making these valuable experiences unique to you.

Companies want experts and innovators: for example, experts at what makes stock markets rise, experts at computer technology, and experts in leadership. To become the expert, even if it involves what seems to be general skills, ask for and attempt to fill new roles and responsibilities. Take on all that you can in a balanced way to fulfill a purpose. Become a contributor, a producer, someone people can trust to get the work done. Be the best you can be for the company, knowing that the day you stop learning is the day you'll take a step back and allow another person to gain one more day of the knowledge you missed.

Knowledge is power. Think about this: As you organize a copy room, you now know where everything is. You become the "expert" of the organization of the copy room. More people will come to you for help finding things in the copy room. There are multiple benefits to this, one of which is that it gives you more face time with your superiors, proving you are truly involving yourself in every part of the business. Look forward to the future as each day becomes an opportunity to improve and learn. Even experts in their field are always learning more and, because they stay up to date, they can stay the "expert." Notice that staying the "expert" involves mental expansion with continuing education from new experiences.

An asset knows what works and what doesn't within the organization. They know how to work and maximize their time. They are organized, needed, and give more value back to their employer.

Finally, don't forget to find at least a particle of exuberance in the work you do. I personally hope you feel at least a little bit excited each day to go in and become an important asset for the company. Let's be real: If you don't, that's okay too – this is only an internship!

The End from the Beginning

Internships are about finding out what you want and learning how to best arrive at your desired "dream job." As much as you want to work for Morgan Stanley, suppose you get there and don't like the work. This happens all the time. If it happens to you, you're not alone. See this time as a masterful study, a time for refining passions. It's important at this early stage in your career to learn a bit about everything before specializing in any one particular thing. It may take you four or five different careers.

Your dreams of a career path can change day in and day out. You never know what's around the corner, so don't be too surprised by anything. Work hard, stay focused, and don't you dare ask the other interns out (very unprofessional). Accept and allow constructive criticism, especially using the expertise of others to guide you. Most importantly, find your path along the journey of your internship(s).

Remember the steps discussed in the earlier chapters, keeping in mind these are suggestions with the goal to help you improve. Try two or three and mold them to your own character. From the beginning: if you choose to clean an office space don't forget to label everything, making it easier to find things later. Be sure you request permission before cleaning and organizing any part of your office. You may not like the way the space looks visually, but it may be a result of someone else's conscious effort. The last thing you want to do is to move things around and cause a commotion. Whatever it is, take this principle to heart: always ask before you do.

When you volunteer for an event or luncheon ask specific details - such as arrival time, preparational tasks, and other relevant information - to ensure you are, as people say, "on the ball." As you become familiar with each individual, realize the best way to talk to them based on their personality style. What do they enjoy about the work they do? What motivates them at work? What helps them do a good job? Do the dirty work, not because you must, but because you choose to, understanding that with every passing day the challenges of the so-called "dirty work" will lessen.

Often, we think we know our niche then find out it's completely different from what we envisioned for ourselves. Be flexible. Allow the ebbs and flows of your thoughts and plans to adjust as you learn. This can be frightening but choose not to fear.

Finally, become the asset you truly are meant to be. Show your passion for an understanding of the business. Gain the knowledge of things that others may think unnecessary and be a sponge of new information. Show your value as you contribute to the overall goals and mission of the organization. Every internship, especially those that guide you to a career, requires diligent and careful work. Some days you may enjoy the scheduled meetings while other days you may enjoy the lunch break. Whatever you do, become the intern you want to become.

As always: I'm here for you, reach out anytime.

P.S. Set yourself up to succeed by taking full responsibility for your own future.

P.P.S. Learn from mistakes and hold on tight. It's going to be a wild ride.

Good luck out there!

Notes/Doodle Page

ACKNOWLEDGMENTS

I had every willing soul I could think of read this text with new ideas and additions after every round of feedback. Admittedly, I decided to write this out of spite, because I thought I hated writing. Fortunately, I showed the text to a variety of people gathering thoughts and learning how to best present them in terms others would understand. There are so many people to thank but I'd like to specifically name a few: My warmest thanks go to my editor and father Dr. John P. Hoffmann and my mother Lynn M. Hoffmann for taking the time to read through and edit any grammatical errors along with correcting some early-draft word choices I would have otherwise dismissed. Big thanks to one of my closest friends, Devin Graham, CEO of Devin Super Tramp, for writing the foreword. A large thanks to the most creative people I personally know who read through and gave me feedback including: Zane O'Gwin, Creighton Baird, Johnny Quintana, Fernando Cutz, Megan Graham, Sherra Swapp, Chris Hoffmann, and Theodore Weiss. Gratefully, they said yes to my many emailed requests and allowed me to use some of their precious time to help guide this project. I hope you, the reader, will find a helpful or insightful idea (or two) to improve your professional career. May this book lead to continuing opportunities for the future.

Notes/Doodle Page

Notes/Doodle Page

About the Author

Brandon Hoffmann is a former professional intern based in College Park, Maryland. Brandon began his work-life before he hit his teenage years, volunteering at the local theater selling concessions, working his way up to the paid facilities staff by his mid-teenage years. At age 16, he pursued a career in facilities management, overseeing the cleanliness of the SCERA Shell Outdoor theater and staffing the SCERA indoor theater. After the summer of 2014, Brandon became an intern with the media production company Devin Super Tramp. Within a few months he took over his first project learning the new 360-degree video technology. After finishing his junior year in high school, he worked his way up to a full-time professional filmmaker, enjoying the fast-paced environment of the social media content revolution. In 2016, Brandon graduated from Mountainland Technical College with a certification in Medical Assisting. Upon completion, he served as an extern specializing in family medicine. After almost 5 years with Devin Super Tramp, Brandon decided to switch things up, moving to the Washington, D.C. area to start as an executive assistant and office manager at Alcoa's Office of Government Affairs and Sustainability until a company-wide lay-off a few months later. Following a 3-week vacation, Brandon found a new position as an executive assistant at The Cohen Group and continues to utilize all the knowledge accumulated during his intern years.

Made in the USA
Middletown, DE
26 February 2020